SS NIEUW AMSTERDAM

The Darling of the Dutch

The *Nieuw Amsterdam* on her maiden arrival into New York. (J&C McCutcheon Collection)

SS NIEUW AMSTERDAM

The Darling of the Dutch

WILLIAM H. MILLER

AMBERLEY

To Vincent Messina

A great ship enthusiast and historian, and who loved and cherished the Nieuw Amsterdam

Amongst ship buffs, particularly ocean liner enthusiasts and historians, I find many have a fascination for a particular ship. Fellow authors Charles Haas and John Eaton, as classic examples, are thoroughly passionate about the immortal *Titanic*. Similarly, marine artist Stephen Card penned a biography of his favorite liner, the *Queen of Bermuda*, while maritime historians Maurizio Eliseo and Paolo Piccione simply adore the Italian liners. Arnold Kludas especially loves the German liners just as Hisashi Noma has the highest interest in Japanese passenger ships. The late Vincent Messina was madly and passionately in love with the *Nieuw Amsterdam*. Although an American, he had in fact a furious passion for almost all things Dutch. He made numerous trips to Holland, had many friends there and often sailed on the good ships of the Holland America Line. Befittingly, he made several trips, beginning in the late 1960s, aboard the glorious *Nieuw Amsterdam*. He all but adopted what he called 'his Darling [of the Dutch]'. He also collected all materials from that ship, studied her history and prepared a superb slide presentation on her life and times. One day, he might even have written his own book on the ship. Sadly, however, he passed away in February 2003, at age fifty-two and surely much too young. But his legacy, his great interest in the *Nieuw Amsterdam*, lives on. It is, therefore, with great regard and deep respect that this book is dedicated to his memory.

First published 2010

Amberley Publishing Plc
Cirencester Road, Chalford,
Stroud, Gloucestershire, GL6 8PE
www.amberley-books.com

Copyright © William H. Miller 2010

The right of William H. Miller to be identified as the Author of this work has been asserted in accordance with the Copyrights, Designs and Patents Act 1988.

ISBN 978 1 84868 366 2

British Library Cataloguing in Publication Data.

A catalogue record for this book is available from the British Library.

Typeset in 10pt on 12pt Sabon.
Typesetting and Origination by Fonthill.
Printed in the UK.

CONTENTS

ACKNOWLEDGEMENTS

Like manning a great liner, it takes many hands – like crew members manning a vessel – to create a book such as this. They too are passionate about ocean liners and this extends to their great generosity in sharing anecdotes and reflections, and providing and even loaning highly valuable materials including prized photos. My full appreciation to each of them! If I have overlooked anyone, my apologies in advance, but greatest thanks to the likes of the late Frank O. Braynard, Jerry and Lorraine Cagiao (the family of Vincent Messina), Stephen Card, Richard Faber, Nico Guns, Michael Hadgis, Pine Hodges, Charles Howland, Anthony La Forgia, Robert Neal Marshall, Captain James McNamara, the late Vincent Messina, Abe Michaelson, the late C. M. Squarey, the late Cees Tensen, Captain Hans van Biljouw, Captain Frederick van Driel, the late Captain Kornelius van Herk, the late Everett Viez, Albert Wilhelmi and Tim Yoder. Other fine assistance came from R. Louis Bafferding, Tom Cassidy, Harley Crossley, Hans de Jong, Anna Kruit, Hisashi Noma, Robert O'Brien, David Rulon, the late William Seabrook, Der Scutt, Captain Ed Squire, the late Everett Viez and the late Joe Wilhelm. Companies and organizations that have assisted include Holland America Line, Moran Towing & Transportation Co., the Steamship Historical Society of America (especially the Long Island, New York chapter), Wilton-Fijenoord Shipyard, World Ocean & Cruise Liner Society and the World Ship Society (especially the Port of New York Branch).

FOREWORD

In 1838, the rival steamships *Sirius* and *Great Western* furiously paddled their way across the North Atlantic, marking the commencement of scheduled trans-Atlantic crossings. Exactly 100 years later, Holland America Line would commemorate this century of progress with what many consider the ultimate Atlantic ocean liner in the form of the *Nieuw Amsterdam*. Her handsome, twin-funneled profile of raked stem and cruiser stern would define the modern ocean liner 'look' for well over a generation – an image so strong that it is today part of the Holland America corporate logo.

Touted as the 'Ship of Tomorrow', 'Ship of Peace', 'Queen of the Spotless Fleet', the Second World War forced her to become a 'Ship of War' and one whose sterling service contributed to the demise of the sinister Axis powers by the Allies and forever cemented the status in the Netherlands as the true 'Darling of the Dutch'. Throughout her long life, spanning almost four decades, she performed all of her roles with a grace that only increased her popularity as a deluxe ocean liner and cruise ship. Designed with a compact, economical power plant that allowed her to cruise at over 20 knots and an extensive mail and cargo capacity, her true glory was her superlative passenger accommodation – a decorative tour de force! At her introduction in 1938, her standard of luxury for all three passenger classes met or exceeded the standard set by much larger ships of that era and beyond. Her impressive *Normandie*-like sweep of moderne extra and double-height public rooms in first class left little to be desired. Second class, with its exceptionally high ratio of staterooms with private facilities, would ensure her popularity as a deluxe liner. The

designated third class was likely the biggest surprise – it approximated the first class of contemporary liners instead of those of decades past. For the first time, this class could enjoy a large variety of public rooms (some air-conditioned!). A grand piano, properly enclosed promenades, the ability to book a single cabin or even one with private facilities! Wonder of wonders – one could even take an unprecedented dip in the swimming pool!

My initial introduction to the fabulous *Nieuw Amsterdam* was as a child growing up in central Africa in the mid-1960s. She was featured in the first ship book I ever bought with my saved pocket money. While I was impressed by her external beauty, at an early age I was attracted, even dazzled, by the larger, more famous trans-Atlantic liners. In this very twilight of the great era of Atlantic liners, I was fortunate enough to return to America onboard the legendary *United States*, seeing an equally large number of soon-to-be-extinct legendary liners in Capetown, Southampton and New York.

The *Nieuw Amsterdam* would become my favorite ship nearly two decades later. Ironically, it would be a Bill Miller book that would ignite a burning desire to find out everything I could about this remarkable ship. At the top of page 110 of *The Great Luxury Liners, 1927-54* was a superb aerial view of the *Nieuw Amsterdam* at her Hoboken, New Jersey pier. I thought then (and still do!) that she was the most beautiful ocean liner I had ever seen. Further reinforcing this view at the bottom of the page was a view of the ship in drab, wartime, troopship gray. Even in that grim, dangerous time and unattractive color, her startling beauty could not be denied!

Shortly afterwards, I had the pleasure to meet Bill Miller on the *Rotterdam* of 1959. He encouraged me in my quest for more information about the ship and introduced me to the late Vincent Messina, who truly was 'Mr *Nieuw Amsterdam*'. Ocean liner researchers such as Vincent and James Kalafus, a marine artist, were generous with their time and collections to satisfy my curiosity.

So, it is with great pleasure and excitement that I learned that my friend Bill Miller was writing and producing a book on this great ship. His ability to find obscure, rare photographs as well as entertaining, enlightening passenger and crew anecdotes is unmatched. This book not only introduces this remarkable ship to the general public, and thrills ship buffs like myself, but will also give her the 'due' she deserves regarding her significant place in trans-Atlantic history.

The *Nieuw Amsterdam* lived a long, productive, profitable life. Born in a worldwide financial depression (not unlike today's times), she reflected the resilience of that great fictional character Auntie Mame. From chic ingénue to sleek, glamorous woman of the world, she finally became a regal, much beloved grande dame of the North Atlantic. She was kept up to date by a company and a crew and clientele that loved her. Like many animate as well as inanimate objects, she probably had her detractors, but I've just never met any of them. In the mid-1980s, I encountered this fierce passion in the form of a feisty widow aboard an eastbound trans-Atlantic crossing on the *Queen Elizabeth 2*. When I asked her why, she firmly declared, 'The *Nieuw Amsterdam* was the personification of graciousness!'

Tim Yoder
Louisville, Ohio
Spring 2010

The *Nieuw Amsterdam* as a troop ship, her dummy aft funnel being most obvious in this view. (J&C McCutcheon Collection)

INTRODUCTION

I began watching the great liners, amidst all else in the great Port of New York, in earnest in the 1950s. Of course, there were also the freighters, the tugs, the ferryboats, but passenger ships were the most intriguing to me. At best, I followed their movements, their comings and goings, in the daily shipping schedules of the *New York Times* and the New York edition of the *Herald Tribune*. There seemed to be, at this distance in time, great order in it all. The legendary Cunard Queens usually arrived on Tuesdays, stayed overnight and then sailed on Wednesdays, always from the north side of Pier 90, at West 50th Street in Manhattan and dead center in the section known as 'Luxury Liner Row'. But other Cunarders such as the *Britannic* and the sisters *Media* and *Parthia* arrived on Saturdays and then did not sail until as long as six days later, on Fridays. In all, I could easily plot my visits to the Hoboken waterfront, just across from the New York City piers, and then watch, say, the *Queen of Bermuda* outbound on Saturday afternoons.

But closer to home, on 'my side' of the Hudson, the Holland America Line had its terminal, two separate piers in fact, at the foot of 5th and 6th Streets, and its own pattern for arrivals and departures. The smaller combo ships *Noordam* and *Westerdam* came and went on Mondays and then sailed on Saturdays. But the big liners like the *Nieuw Amsterdam* and *Statendam* arrived on Wednesday mornings and then sailed on Friday afternoons. (The larger *Rotterdam* actually rotated with that pair, but arrived on Tuesday afternoons and then sailed on Friday afternoons.) It was on these occasions that I often saw the beautiful *Nieuw Amsterdam*, berthed on the south side of that 5th Street pier. She was big, always impeccable and, to my young eye, already one of my top favorite liners. Without any doubt, she was one of the most beautiful liners of her time. She was also the embodiment of the great, romanticized ocean liner. She was pure perfection, pure high style, pure sea-going poetry. It is, therefore, both a great honor and privilege to document this great Dutch lady's life and times. And in creating this tribute, it might once again be Hoboken in the 1950s, the Holland America Line piers and, most especially, the *Nieuw Amsterdam* at berth.

Bill Miller
Secaucus, New Jersey
Spring 2010

Vincent Messina, known as 'Mr *Nieuw Amsterdam*', photographed on the rooftop deck of Holland America Line's Pier 40 at New York in 1967. (Vincent Messina Collection)

The *Nieuw Amsterdam* leaving Southampton on 19 June 1968. (J&C McCutcheon Collection)

HIGH SPIRITS: CREATING A NEW NATIONAL FLAGSHIP

The *Nieuw Amsterdam* was, and remains in memory to this day, one of the finest, most beloved and endearing ocean liners ever commissioned. Her 'soul' was one which attached itself to loyal fans, both ashore and afloat, and has probably made her the best-known Dutch ship of the twentieth century. To ocean liner purists, she was one of a selected two dozen or so ships that came close to perfection in both overall exterior design and interior decoration.

She was conceived from the beginning to be the national flagship, the biggest yet built in Holland and something of a tour de force of decorative splendor and modernity. However, Holland America found itself blessed even further: she promptly became one of the very few, highly profitable larger liners of the 1930s, developing an almost instant love affair with the traveling public.

In the mid-1930s, despite the bleak economic climate, big ships as well as national ships – the 'ships of state' as they were commonly known – were very much in the wind. The Germans had their 50,000-ton near-sisters *Bremen* and *Europa* from 1929-30; the Italians had the 51,000-ton *Rex* and her running-mate, the 48,000-ton *Conte di Savoia*, both from 1932; the French produced their magnificent 83,000-ton *Normandie* by 1935, which was followed almost immediately by Britain's *Queen Mary*, at 81,000 tons, in 1936. Holland was not to be left out. However, the Holland America Line, as owners of such a projected ship, did not think of having the world's largest or fastest ship (distinctions that several of the aforementioned had actually rivaled for). Instead, while assuredly to be the largest liner yet under the Dutch flag as well as the largest built on

home soil, she would be in fact more medium sized, more moderate, at some 36,000 tons.

The company's proposal to build a new flagship came in 1935, just at the time when the trans-Atlantic trade had dropped by some 50 per cent and when forecasts were far from encouraging. However, such a new national flagship was not simply to be a money-spinner. She was, above all else, to be a floating symbol of national art, technology and decoration. In short, she would be the finest moving representative of her country. Secondly, her creation and construction were looked upon as a tonic, a morale boost in an otherwise hard-pressed era at home. Thirdly, she offered further employment to shipyard crews, design teams and engineers, and a worried staff at Holland America. (There had been rumors hinting of Holland America's collapse during the severe earlier 1930s.) Further, the company (and the nation) wanted at least the indulgence to follow and even mildly compete with the British, French and others with their new liner creations.

The company had some financial reserves, but government loans were absolutely essential before the building order could be signed and construction begun. Of course, an important element was that she would be built at home, in Holland, unlike all of the earlier company liners which had come from Belfast in Northern Ireland. Happily, an agreement was reached, and the first keel plates were laid in position in January 1936.

It had been intended, almost from the start, that the new ship would bear a name not yet used by Holland America. The selection was *Prinsendam*. However, as the great hull began to take shape, there was some rethinking on the matter and it was decided that *Nieuw Amsterdam* was a far more appropriate choice. After all, the liner would sail from Holland to New York and then on cruises from that American port as well. It was the perfect friendly gesture. Historically, New York had once been the tiny Dutch settlement of New Amsterdam.

The builders of the ship, the Rotterdam Dry Dock Company, fixed the cost of the new liner at 13,500,000 guilders. However, the structure of the financing was tight. The shipyard workers responded with a voluntary 2 ½ per cent wage cut. Thus, it was claimed that the new *Nieuw Amsterdam* was paid for by the government, by the company and by the people.

Furthermore, the ship has a rather unique status in the annals of twentieth century ocean liners. 'She has a special place in history equal in ways to the two giant Cunard Queens,' commented passenger ship enthusiast and historian Pine Hodges. 'This is due in parts because she survived World War II, carrying a half-million troops, often in convoy with the likes of those big Queens, because she is the first large liner to be built in a Dutch shipyard, and because she was the flagship of the once-huge Dutch merchant marine.'

The *Nieuw Amsterdam* has had legions of fans. Ocean liner expert Charles Howland is among them and said, 'I always loved the *Nieuw Amsterdam* for her good looks. She had a four-square stance that radiated strength and sea-worthiness. The curve of her bridge front was both graceful and strong, which lead the eye aft to the neat and unbroken line of promenade deck windows. These elements combined with her simple teardrop-shaped stacks created a well-balanced and charming profile. If ever a design shouted classic ocean liner, the *Nieuw Amsterdam*'s did.

'I think it is interesting to compare the *Nieuw Amsterdam*'s profile and interior layout to two other near-contemporary liners, the transcendent *Normandie* of 1935 and William Francis Gibbs' masterpiece *America* of 1939,' added Howland. 'All three ships shared a common exterior design element. They all sported dummy funnels. In the case of the *Normandie*, her third funnel housed the ship's kennels and dog run. On the *America*, her forward stack was a dummy that gave balance and a certain majesty to her profile. In the *Nieuw Amsterdam*'s case, it was the aft funnel that was the dummy. Ship designers of the era seem to have cared very much about their ship's profile – to the point of adding these large faux smokestacks where, mechanically speaking, none were required. It is a good thing they did, however, because each of these magnificent liners could never be mistaken for any other. And that, probably, is precisely the point.

'The *Nieuw Amsterdam* shared another trait with the *Normandie*,' continued Howland, who maintains a state-of-the-art ocean liner collection in his Manhattan apartment. 'Ship lovers are always quick to point out how divided boiler casings gave the French ship's interior designers the opportunity to create the magnificent central vistas that characterized her public rooms. What isn't so well known is that the designers of the *Nieuw Amsterdam* did the same thing. Her funnel casing was also divided, allowing for a dramatic main staircase and entrance to the first-class lounge and rooms beyond.'

World-class ocean liner collector and noted architect Der Scutt had added comments on the design, creation and overall beauty of the *Nieuw Amsterdam*. 'When the *Nieuw Amsterdam* was designed in the first half of the 1930s, the influence of the impeccable *Normandie* on the Dutch ship was clearly evident. Of particular significance was the promenade deck banding, which continued from the slides around the front without clutter in a single, bold form. The *Nieuw Amsterdam* was also one of the last ships of the era to have the foremast on the foredeck. Also, the layering of the decks generated from the sheer curvature contributed to the streamlining of the hull's mass. The upper part of the ship provided an abundance of deck space for outdoor sports, sunbathing and other open-air enjoyments. I did think, however, painting her hull gray in later years was a terrible mistake, primarily because it lessened the impressive character of the ship. Somehow, being an everyday cruise liner was no substitution for this grand Dutch dame with its sophisticated dark hull. Ladies attending a formal gala do not wear spring clothes, no matter what time of year!'

The *Nieuw Amsterdam* docked in the Western Docks, Southampton, 19 June 1968. (J&C McCutcheon Collection)

II

HOLLAND AMERICA: A GRAND HISTORY

Indeed, Holland America has great history. In 2003, for example, the company reached a milestone: 130 years of continuous service. Beginning in 1873, the 1,700-ton *Rotterdam,* the first of many to bear that illustrious name, was the pioneer ship that has led to fourteen cruise liners by 2009. An 86,000-tonner, the *Nieuw Amsterdam*, joins in 2010. The roots of the company go back to a Dutch firm, Plate, Reuchlin & Company, formed in 1871, but which soon ran into financial troubles and so had to be reorganized two years later as the Netherlands American Steamship Company, NASM, or the Holland America Line. The fleet thereafter grew quickly, and a regular service developed on the Atlantic, between Rotterdam and New York City (they moved across the Hudson River to Hoboken in 1890), later regularly including ports in England, France and Ireland. Regularity and reliability became two of the company's trademarks – and added to its popularity and profitability. Holland America ships grew in size, speed and passenger comfort, and the number of Atlantic sailings increased steadily.

By the turn of the century, the Atlantic was in a peak period and Holland America prospered further. Their ships carried, as an example, over 5 per cent of the 18 million immigrants that crossed to America, to the 'New World', between 1892 and 1924. After 1924, the US placed major immigration quotas on the inbound flow. Reflecting the boom period, the 12,500-ton *Noordam*, completed in 1902, carried 2,300 passengers in total – 300 in first class, 200 in second class, and then a hefty 1,800 in third class or steerage. Earlier, in 1898, the company's twenty-fifth anniversary records were already quite impressive: 500,000 passengers carried in total, of which 90,000 were in first and second class, and over 400,000 in lower-

deck steerage. Then there was also 5,000,000 tons of freight (flower bulbs, herring and gin). Holland America added its first pure freighter in 1901 and, expanding beyond North Atlantic passenger sailings, ran its first all-one-class, luxury cruise onboard the 10,000-ton *Statendam*, which sailed to the Mediterranean and the Holy Land in 1910.

A largely conservative company in many ways, Holland America was, for example, not quite convinced of the overall reliability of steam turbine propulsion. The 17,000-ton *Nieuw Amsterdam* of 1906 was the last Atlantic liner to include sails as possible alternate power. Two years later, in 1908, the company added its largest liner yet, the 24,000-ton *Rotterdam*, a fine-looking twin-stacker that could carry 3,555 passengers in three classes.

Holland America also endured periodic slumps, two world wars and the hard times following the Wall Street Crash in October 1929. In the First World War, the company lost over a dozen ships. The new flagship *Statendam*, under construction at a Belfast shipyard, was commandeered by the British Government before completion and instead fitted out as the troopship *Justicia*. Sadly, her days were numbered. The 32,000-ton ship sank in July 1918.

The company lost millions in the early 1930s – reducing the fleet, prematurely scrapping other ships and cutting staff. In ways, and with Atlantic liner travel down by 50 per cent by 1935, Holland America was forced to survive on the likes of $50 per person, week-long cruises to Bermuda, Nassau or Havana. They did manage to produce a beautiful new flagship, the *Statendam*, in 1929. Although a very traditional liner both inside and out, she had, according to one appraisal, some of the finest interiors of all Atlantic liners of her time. 'The main ballroom actually resembled a state ballroom from a French chateau. Paneled, carved-oak walls extended two decks in height and were embellished with a magnificent, hand-loomed Gobelin tapestry. Nearby, the smoking room, adjoining the bar, was nothing short of baronial in its subdued splendor. Onboard, there were also fixtures in polished brass, domed glass skylights, imposing fireplaces, veined marble and colored tile. The indoor swimming pool was constructed, in fact, almost entirely of Dutch tiles, while a constant flow of pre-heated saltwater kept the facility at a comfortable temperature.'

But even in the financially worrisome mid-1930s, with the Depression far from over, Holland America commissioned one of the finest ocean liners of the day. The *Nieuw Amsterdam*, completed in May 1938, was pure dreamboat.

Opposite, top: The stately *Rotterdam* of 1908, at berth at the Wilhelminakade at Rotterdam. (Richard Faber Collection)

Right: Popular ships of the early 1920s, the sisters *Veendam* and *Volendam* (shown here at Rotterdam in September 1938), gave long service to the company. (Albert Wilhelmi Collection)

The *Veendam* on her final visit to New York in October 1953. She is seen at Holland America Line's 5th Street pier in Hoboken. (Richard Faber Collection)

The twin funnels of the *Volendam* as seen in the late 1940s. (Richard Faber Collection)

Looking like a larger liner, the 8,800-ton *Maasdam* of 1921 plied the North Europe-Gulf of Mexico service. (Richard Faber Collection)

Above left: The classic-looking *Statendam* was commissioned in 1929. (Albert Wilhelmi Collection)

Above right: Holland America cruising in the 1930s: the *Statendam* is seen at Rhodes during a long Mediterranean cruise. (Albert Wilhelmi Collection)

Left: Holland America liner in New York harbor in the 1890s. (Stephen Card Collection)

Right Holland America Line posters from the 1890s. (J&c McCutcheon Collection)

A painting of the *Veendam* from the 1920s. (Holland America Line)

Above: A glorious view: the *Statendam* arriving off Lower Manhattan in an evening setting. (Stephen Card Collection)

Right: The latest flagship, the *Statendam* of 1929. (Holland America Line)

Famed French artist Cassandre created a very special poster in 1929 for Holland America Line, highlighting the *Statendam*'s three funnels. (Holland America Line)

A baggage tag from the 1920s. (Holland America Line)

III

JUBILATION AND CONFETTI: MAIDEN YEARS 1938-39

The *Nieuw Amsterdam* was one of the grandest of the floating palaces. The 36,000-ton, 1,220-passenger flagship was, among other styles, done in cherished Art Deco – and in its highest form. 'The *Nieuw Amsterdam* was just about as close to ocean liner perfection as you can get,' said the late Everett Viez, an ocean liner historian who began sailing on passenger ships in the late 1920s. 'On the outside, she was incredibly handsome – two gently raked smokestacks perfectly balanced upon an all-white superstructure set between two towering masts and a yellow stripe around the black-painted (later gray) hull. But on the inside, she was a masterpiece. Gorgeous Art Deco interiors, décor and objects d'art complemented some of the more traditional Dutch styles, fittings and furnishings. There were richly polished woods, gleaming stainless and the likes of exotic ebony and Makassar woods. Her main dining room was quite stunning and had Murano chandeliers set against a Moroccan leather ceiling. The columns were gilded in gold tiling and there was a balcony for an orchestra that overlooked the two-deck high restaurant. Service in that first-class setting was, of course, beyond compare – waiters in perfectly pressed uniforms, impeccable manners and rich Dutch charm. No wonder that the *Nieuw Amsterdam* was one of the most popular and profitable liners on the Atlantic. She well deserved her subsequent nickname – "the Darling of the Dutch".'

Journalist R. Louis Bofferding wrote, in a reflection on ocean liner design and décor in a 2008 article in *Elle Decor,* that 'the world economy had picked up by the end of the decade, so in 1938, the Holland America Line launched the *Nieuw Amsterdam,* whose interiors had an easy elegance that reflected the modern movement. And if the typical passenger of the day wasn't keen on the Dutch ship's cantilevered glass and tubular steel, the addition of nubby woven fabrics and bias-quilting softened the harshness.'

Heightened preparations and news for the *Nieuw Amsterdam* began in 1936, when her construction began in home waters, at the Rotterdam Dry Dock Company at Rotterdam. Conveniently, the Holland America offices were nearby at the Wilhelminakade. From the start, printed material in English differed slightly from past items. Previously, the Dutch operated a ship bearing the name *Nieuw Amsterdam*, but it was not until the late 1930s, according to the late Frank Braynard, one of the greatest of all ocean liner historians and authors, that the Dutch spelling was used. Before then, 'New' instead of 'Nieuw' was used in deck plans, folders and even sailing schedules.

On an April day in 1937, Queen Wilhelmina christened the *Nieuw Amsterdam*. A huge ship to the Dutch at 36,000 tons, she was noted as a very important benchmark in the annals of Dutch shipbuilding. She was twice as large as any vessel ever before constructed in Holland. But with the nicest motives, there were no elements for possible use in war incorporated into her overall design. Promptly, she was dubbed Holland's 'Ship of Peace'. But just east, in Nazi Germany, Hitler and his ministers were beginning to make plans that would shatter not only European but worldwide peace. Certainly, there were dark times ahead for Holland and a less-than-luxurious role for the *Nieuw Amsterdam* as a wartime trooper. At the time of the launch, the Queen herself raised a glass in toast and said, 'To the common good and safe journey of the new ship, the *Nieuw Amsterdam*, I propose this toast.'

The 758-foot-long *Nieuw Amsterdam* was constructed on the otherwise narrow River Maas, in fact, just opposite from where the tiny sailing ship *Speedwell* set sail for America, the New World, three centuries before. The Rotterdam Dry Dock Company had to plan very carefully, taking great precaution that the hull of the new liner would not crash into the opposite bank of the river at launching. Consequently, ten large braces were welded into the hull and each was fastened to long, heavy anchor chains with an aggregate weight of 1,000 tons. Slung at intervals along her sides, these chains were released two at a time as the *Nieuw Amsterdam* slid down the ways. And it all worked to perfection. Once the liner became fully waterborne, the weight of the chains brought the vessel to a full stop within her own length.

The fitting-out took over a year. Periodic new releases prompted interest and added enthusiasm for the new Dutch flagship. The two 60-ton smokestacks were brought alongside, one at a time, and lifted aboard by a large floating crane. Both Holland America as well as the shipyard noted that the small tug that towed the crane to the ship's side could not only have fitted inside the funnels, but turned around within them as well.

In shipping circles in Holland, and despite the increasingly uncertain situation with the growing forces and vague, but worrisome intentions in Nazi Germany, the Dutch were at something of a peak period. Not only was the *Nieuw Amsterdam* being built for the Holland America Line, but the Nederland Line, one of the strongest companies on the Dutch colonial route out to the East Indies, was also building a new flagship, the 20,500-ton *Oranje*. Meanwhile, another colonial liner company, Rotterdam Lloyd, was planning an even larger ship, a 23,000-tonner, but this would be delayed by the war and become the *Willem Ruys* in 1947.

Ocean liners, especially large ones, were still very much in future planning in the late 1930s. Cunard was busily at work on the 83,000-ton *Queen Elizabeth*, the second of its famed trans-Atlantic Queens, which was due in service in April 1940 (this did not come about, of course, due to the outbreak of war in September 1939). On the heels of the brilliant *Normandie*, the French were rumored to be considering an even larger liner, the 100,000-ton *Bretagne*. Meanwhile, the North German Lloyd was said to be considering re-engining their two record-breaking superliners *Bremen* and *Europa*, and then later rather seriously planning for no less than a 90,000-ton super ship, the *Amerika*. The Hamburg America Line had begun construction on the first of a trio of 41,000-tonners, the *Vaterland*.

More moderately, some medium-sized liners were in the works in the late 1930s as well. Cunard had their 35,000-ton *Mauretania* scheduled for commissioning in the spring of 1939, while across the Atlantic, the United States Lines was building the 33,000-ton *America*, due out in the summer of 1940. In addition, the likes of the Swedish American Line and Norwegian America Line were creating new flagships, the *Stockholm* and the *Oslofjord*.

When completed in the spring of 1938, the *Nieuw Amsterdam* became a ship of great interest on both sides of the Atlantic. Her interiors seemed to attract considerable attention. 'Her interior was a combination of real, but unostentatious luxury and serviceability,' noted Frank Braynard.

Company literature hailed her many distinctions, notations, the thoughtful touches. She was, for example, the only liner in trans-Atlantic service to have either a private bath or shower and toilet in every room in first class. She could carry 556 in first class (then called cabin class), 455 in cabin class (then dubbed tourist class) and 309 in tourist class (then listed as third class). Some 2,000 of her 15,000 lamps were fluorescent tubes for indirect, softer lighting. All the cooking was done by electricity, except for a charcoal grill used for the likes of steaks and chops. Some 3,550 chairs were built for passenger staterooms and the public rooms. There were sixty electric clocks, which were connected to a master clock on the ship's bridge. Amidst her eleven passenger decks, there were 546 passenger cabins, nearly 10,000 square feet of carpeting, 750 tables, ten elevators and an equal number of kennels, and a total of twenty-three public rooms.

Decorating the *Nieuw Amsterdam* was a great achievement as well. Some of her interior stylings were inspired by the Paris World's Fair of 1933 while other portions were so modern that they would be used in the 1939 fair at New York, still well over a year away. Understandably, she was also dubbed 'the ship of tomorrow'. Various metals, glass and, of course, woods were used throughout. In fact, there were twenty-six different types used in the decoration – with names like bird's eye maple, Burma mahogany, silver sycamore, mountain ash, figured cherry, Indian silvergrey, weathered satinwood, makore, Makassar, ebony, bubinga and zebrano.

In first class, there were twelve deluxe suites, which were separately designed and furnished. Each of these rooms had its own entrance-mounted coat of arms and was named after the Dutch provinces as well as overseas colonial outposts: Groningen, Holland, Freisland, Zeeland, Drenthe, Noordbrabant, Overijssel, Limburg, Gelderland, Antillen, Utrecht and Suriname. Each consisted of a sitting room, bedroom, bathroom and wardrobe-dressing room. The color schemes varied – from Chinese red and cream to turquoise and silver.

Other portions of the ship were equally noteworthy and impressive. The first-class restaurant had pilasters of ebony, chairs and tables of Satinwood, scallop-shell ceiling fixtures of Murano glass made especially in Venice. The foyer included two fine oils of New York City and a mounted model of

Henry Hudson's *Half Moon*. The cocktail bar in the Ritz Carlton Lounge was done in Coromandel wood while the Smoking Room had walnut club chairs upholstered in fine leather. Indeed, she was a ship of riches and treasures.

Frank Braynard wrote of the *Nieuw Amsterdam*, 'Her interior decorations were revolutionary in ship design. The Grand Hall boasted a suspended moulded-aluminum ceiling. Two immense murals, virtually the full width of the room, concealed soft artificial lighting. New gray, yellow and green pastel shades were used in abundance, intended to enhance fully the glamorous effect of exquisitely gowned women and their escorts in evening dress. An air-conditioned theater occupied a large portion of the forward promenade deck, unique in that it had absolutely no decoration, being of the utmost simplicity in design.'

Noted skyscraper architect Der Scutt also found the interiors to be very pleasing. He said, 'Whereas the British, Germans and Italians were all exploring new concepts of interior design, either with Classicism or Art Nouveau Riche, the Dutch adhered to creating simple, comfortable and elegant interiors of the time. Spaciousness, with fine appointments, along with craftsmanship and a variety of color and décor, was always inviting, but never ostentatious. The designers did flirt with Art Deco, but with repression. There was little bric-à-brac or flamboyant visual fanfare dangling about. Restrained design manners prevailed.

'The dining rooms were handsomely proportioned spaces, for example,' added Scutt, 'a combination of tinted mirrors, soft diffused lighting and plush materials, muted in color, created an air of distinction. Dining in a peaceful environment is essential. One doesn't want to be taunted with frolicking and dancing sparkle. Quite simply, it is not conducive to healthy digestion! The best landside restaurants with the best food all thrive in simple, plain design ambience.'

Charles Howland agreed. 'For sheer sparkle and drama, no ship of the 1930s can compare with the drop-dead flair of the great *Normandie*'s interiors, but the *Nieuw Amsterdam* wasn't far behind. For a Dutch ship, her interiors were a great leap forward. They combined fine wood veneers, highly polished floors where Fred and Ginger would have felt right at home, with a world-class collection of art. Her first-class dining room was the very essence of Art Deco simplicity.

'The traveling public took to the *Nieuw Amsterdam* in a way that they never did with the *Normandie*,' concluded Howland. 'Her interiors, though ultra-modern, must have had a warmth and coziness that appealed to passengers. She developed a loyal following before World War II, amassed an enviable trooping record during the war and, in postwar, her passengers came flooding back. Few ships have ever repaid their owners as fully as the *Nieuw Amsterdam* did.'

Travel writers, design editors and decorative aficionados on both sides of the Atlantic were quick to praise the beauty of the *Nieuw Amsterdam*. Of course, thought was given almost immediately to building a duplicate, a twin sister ship. However, a variety of factors prevented the scheme: the reluctance of further loans from the Dutch Government, a shortage of funds on the part of Holland America Line itself and, even more dramatically, the fast-approaching war clouds.

The *Nieuw Amsterdam* was also highly praised and cherished for her exterior, her all-but-perfect good looks. And along with the superb balance of her raked twin funnels placed between two towering, but also raked masts, the liner had a very pronounced sense of sheer. Der Scutt observed, 'The *Nieuw Amsterdam* had the most pronounced sheer of any ship of its time. The *Kaiser Wilhelm der Grosse* (1897) and other ships had various degrees of sheer, of course. Freeboard, sometimes called sheer, is defined as the height of the side of a ship above the waterline at the middle upper length, measured from the top of the deck at the side, creating a curvature in the deck profiles, where the ship is higher at either end. The idea within naval technology dated from the 1880s with the main objective of supporting the plating and to resist transfer straining forces at the support of the ship's structure against longitudinal strain. Ironically, this sophisticated naval technology added to the charm and beauty of the *Nieuw Amsterdam*'s profile. Somehow, the curvature of the decks, especially at the waterline, signaled a harmonious kissing of the waves with a big broad smile. It also implied speed.'

Within a year, by 1939, the *Nieuw Amsterdam* established herself not only as a very popular liner, but one of the most profitable ships in the world.

Also, by the late 1930s, in addition to their year-round crossings to and from northern Europe, to/from Southampton, Le Havre and Rotterdam, Holland America offered a twelve-month roster of one-class pleasure cruises. Travelers had diverse offerings – from five days to Bermuda on the *Veendam*, with rates from $60; to seventeen days around the Caribbean on the *Volendam*, from $135; forty-two days throughout the Mediterranean on the *Statendam*, from $400; and, a special event, a month-long trip to Rio for the annual carnival on the brand-new *Nieuw Amsterdam*, from $350. But by the summer of 1939, the political situation in Europe was beginning to change. Like a descending summertime storm, war clouds were forming.

While at her berth at the 5th Street pier in Hoboken, early in September 1939, the *Nieuw Amsterdam* was altered slightly. Huge neutrality

markings were painted along her sides. Soon afterward, and after only seventeen and a half voyages on the Atlantic, it was decided that the North Atlantic was far too uncertain, even unsafe for the new Dutch flagship. She was laid-up at her Hoboken pier. Across the Hudson, other liners, such as the *Queen Mary* and *Normandie*, were also waiting, caught in a deepening limbo. Then, in the spring of 1940, she was reactivated. But quite sensibly, she was kept in safer waters – cruising steadily from New York to Bermuda, the Bahamas and the Caribbean.

Above: Detail from an Art Deco poster of the *Statendam*. (J&C McCutcheon Collection)

Left: The cover of the official launch program.

Presentation: flowers for Her Majesty Queen Wilhelmina.

The largest vessel yet constructed in the Netherlands: an aerial view of the hull prior to launching.

A dramatic aerial view from one of the shipyard cranes of the Queen's arrival at the Rotterdam Dry Dock Company yard, in April 1937. (all photos this page, Nico Guns Collection)

Above left: The much-needed drag chains, which will stop the liner in her own length on the otherwise-narrow River Maas.

Above right: The Queen, along with Holland America Line, government and shipyard officials, as seen beneath the towering bow.

Left: The royal mallet, which will be used to release the christening wine.

Above left: Her Majesty has named the ship and releases the christening wine.

Above right: The new liner is very nearly fully afloat.

Right: And now fully afloat and in her element! (all photos these two pages, Nico Guns Collection)

Above left: The great hull of the 36,000-ton flagship, Holland's new pride of the seas.

Above right: A view from the bow section of the otherwise incomplete liner.

Left: Tugboat assistance and guidance for the otherwise powerless liner.

Above left: The great bow as the liner is shifted to the fitting-out berth.

Above right: At the fitting-out berth. The final fitting-out of the liner will begin in a day's time.

Right: Guests depart and complete the day's festivities. (all photos these two pages, Nico Guns Collection)

Above left: An early postcard view of the beautiful *Nieuw Amsterdam*. (Albert Wilhelmi Collection)

Above right: A commemorative envelope of the liner's maiden voyage in May 1938. (Albert Wilhelmi Collection)

Below left: Nearing completion in this view from spring 1938. (Richard Faber Collection)

Above left: Tugs handle the 758-foot-long liner. (Vincent Messina Collection)

Above right: An arrival in New York harbor in 1939. (Author's Collection)

Right: Triumphant and gleaming: the new flagship arrives off Lower Manhattan in late afternoon sunshine. The classic Woolworth Building is to the left. (Albert Wilhelmi Collection)

A grand gathering at the Wilhelminakade in 1938: the *Volendam* (left), the *Statendam* (center) and the *Nieuw Amsterdam* (right). (Holland America Line)

Another view of the three liners at Rotterdam. (Albert Wilhelmi Collection)

An aerial view of the maiden arrival – with the Empire State Building just to the left of center. The cruise ship *Oriente* is berthed to the right of the inbound *Nieuw Amsterdam*. (Albert Wilhelmi Collection)

Right: Departure from Hoboken in 1938. (Frank O. Braynard Collection)

Below: A poster highlighting the debut of the *Nieuw Amsterdam*. (Holland America Line)

Above: The *Nieuw Amsterdam* docking at Hoboken. (Frank O. Braynard Collection)

Left: A brochure cover from the 1950s. (Holland America Line)

IV

GRAY PAINT: WARTIME ON THE HIGH SEAS

On a winter morning, but in high, very warm sunshine, in 2009, our cruise ship arrived at Willemstad on Curacao. The island's buildings were bright and well painted, tour buses lined the quayside and, for some, the shops, the restaurants, the museums and the sandy beaches beckoned. Curacao plays a part in the story of the *Nieuw Amsterdam*, but in the tense days of May 1940. The Second World War had started in Europe, following the fierce Nazi invasion of smaller, innocent Poland in September 1939. Fearing attacks by sinister Nazi U-boats, which were already prowling the Northern seas, the Holland America Line decided to keep the *Nieuw Amsterdam* in far safer waters, cruising tranquil Bermuda, the Bahamas and the Caribbean. While the war's course in Europe was uncertain, a dramatic chapter unfolded in May 1940. The Nazis attacked the Low Countries. Holland was under siege, being invaded by the ferocious German armies.

In May 1940, Holland was still at peace, the Nazis were having trouble with Norway and the so-called 'phoney war' was still being talked about. On May 10th, no less than six Holland America Line vessels were lying at berth at Rotterdam. There were the liners *Statendam* and *Veendam* as well as the cargo vessels *Damsterdyk*, *Drechtdyk*, *Dinteldyk* and *Boschdyk*. That same day, Nazi forces slipped over the Dutch border and began their invasion. Four days later, Rotterdam was subjected to one of the most intense bombings in history. Holland America had attempted to move most or all of the six ships, but the Germans had already blocked the harbor with magnetic mines. Consequently, some of the worst fighting took place in and around the Wilhelminakade and the grand, three-funnel *Statendam* was caught in the crossfire from both sides of the River Maas,

caught fire and then burned for no less than five days. There had been rumors that the Nazis planned to use her as a 'floating fort', but this was later disproved. The Dutch themselves had planned to sink her at the pier, but resisted when thinking of crew members below decks. The 697-foot-long ship was soon a blackened, blistered wreck. Soon she would be towed away, her remains scrapped and the last of her metals dispatched to Nazi munitions plants and steel recycling mills.

Across the sea, in the Caribbean, the *Nieuw Amsterdam* had left Curacao and been to La Guaira in Venezuela where the horrifying news was flashed that the Netherlands had been invaded and was about to fall. The Dutch Government fled into exile and none other than Queen Wilhelmina escaped across the Channel to London, traveling deep in the night and carrying the crown jewels in no less than brown paper bags. The Government-in-exile was soon established aboard the *Westernland*, a Holland America liner that was moored off Falmouth, England, and under the direction of Prince Bernhard, the German-born husband of Crown Princess Juliana.

Holland America's New York office along Lower Broadway ordered the *Nieuw Amsterdam* to return to Hoboken immediately. Leisure cruises to the Caribbean was pushed aside for more pressing duties: using the flagship of the Netherlands as a very valuable, high-capacity Allied troopship. After the passengers were landed at the 5th Street pier in Hoboken, the ship was ordered to Halifax, Nova Scotia, to begin trooping, but only after a quick turn at the Todd Shipyard's graving dock in the Erie Basin, Brooklyn. The 758-foot-long liner was the largest to use the graving dock, barely squeezing into the berth. The outer dock gates had to be left open for the overhang of the bow and the stern. Now painted entirely in gray, the *Nieuw Amsterdam* soon quietly and secretly left for Halifax.

On September 14th, without formal notation, she arrived at the Nova Scotia port. Some of her luxurious fittings and furnishings were sent ashore, dispatched to wartime storage. Hurriedly, her 1,200 or so peacetime berths were reconfigured for as many as 6,000 in extremely crowded wartime conditions. The cinema and the great Grand Hall became large dormitories, all but jammed with tiers of folding steel bunks, some with as little as 3-4 feet between them. Accommodations for eighteen were built into staterooms previously instead for two in peacetime spaciousness. All of C Deck, which had housed cabin- and tourist-class cabins as well as the indoor swimming pool and gymnasium, had been ripped out and instead used for troop berthing. Long benches and wooden tables supplanted cushioned chairs and mahogany tables in the dining rooms. Meals were, of course, a huge task. Two meals per day, breakfast and dinner, were provided during the war years. There was no lunch. Beginning at sunrise and often ending at sunset, there were ten sittings of fifteen minutes each. The dinner sessions usually began at 4.30 in the afternoon.

Provisioning was, of course, an enormous task during the war. Each day, the likes of 240 gallons of milk were consumed along with eighty bags of flour, some 13,000 eggs, 1,000 pounds of bacon, 6,400 quarts of coffee, 14,000 loaves of bread and almost 900 pounds of butter.

Equipped with a degaussing cable and now completely painted in military grays, the *Nieuw Amsterdam* was placed under Allied control, with the British Government, and soon sped off for far-away Singapore via the South African Cape. Some of her luxurious fittings were covered by plywood and others stored in the ship's holds. At Singapore, she was refitted further, receiving extensive armament. Her sumptuous artworks, furniture and other treasures were rather carelessly dumped on the Singapore docks and then left exposed to all kinds of tropical weather, including intense heat and harsh rains. The urgencies of war had far higher priorities. (The fittings were in fact later shipped to Australia, aboard the *Nieuw Amsterdam* herself. Still later, they were sent to San Francisco and kept there until the end of the war in 1945-46, when they were ordered home to Holland by freighter for the ship's postwar refit.) No less than thirty-six guns were now added to her decks. She could, it was estimated, carry over 8,000 at one time in pressing conditions. In all, she would carry 400,000 persons during the war years – and all without incident or accident. She outdid herself and proved to be one of the war's most successful and heroic troopships.

In the early years of the war, the *Nieuw Amsterdam*'s sailings were confined mostly to the Indian Ocean. After completing her troopship conversion at Singapore, she sailed to Sydney and then to Wellington in New Zealand to load her first soldier-passengers. She sailed next to Bombay, in convoy company with such noted former luxury liners as the *Queen Mary*, *Aquitania* and *Mauretania*. Afterward, she made ten trips in something of a 'relay service' between Suez and Durban.

She had her most noted passengers aboard in July 1941, during a voyage south from Suez to Durban. First exiled to Egypt, the *Nieuw Amsterdam* transported the Greek royal family and their entourage to further exile and British protection in South Africa. Aboard were King George II, Crown Prince Paul, Crown Princess Frederika and their two young children, Princess Sophia (today the Queen of Spain) and Prince Constantine (now the Greek king, but living in exile in England). The Greek royals were given cabin accommodations and were provided with meals and service that were almost equal to peacetime standards. Special awards and medals were later given to the senior officers of the *Nieuw Amsterdam* by the Greek king in recognition of the safety and comfort provided.

The ship's commander, Captain George Barendse, said during the war, 'Remember, she is the flagship, the treasure and the queen of the Holland America Line, and she sails with luck.' And indeed she did. Following the Japanese attack on Pearl Harbor and the US entry into the Second World War in December 1941, the *Nieuw Amsterdam* was ordered to the Pacific and made numerous trips from the likes of San Francisco and Los Angeles to ports in New Zealand and Australia. The Pacific was in fact her mainstay for some years.

In early 1943, she was sent to a San Francisco shipyard for further dry docking and refitting. She had been experiencing propeller problems, and at the same time, her official troop capacity had to be increased. Her new wartime certificate was for 6,070, with standee berths having been replaced by wooden bunks. Furthermore, she was fitted with twenty-seven pieces of artillery for her own defense. She returned to a shipyard in San Francisco for a second time, in the autumn of 1943, for additional alterations. Her troop capacity was enlarged once again, this time to 8,065. However, such a figure was often well exceeded.

She did not return to New York until May 1944, when she was placed on the great North Atlantic troop shuttle, and in company with the likes of the giant Cunard Queens as well as the French *Ile de France* and *Pasteur*, between New York and Gourock in Scotland. Her sailings were made in preparation for the Normandy Invasion. She crossed with both

American and Canadian servicemen, mostly used a far northern route and also made a single sailing down to Liverpool.

When at her Hoboken pier on that first return visit in May 1944, she had a special visitor. While living in Canada in wartime exile, Princess Juliana, heiress to the Dutch throne, visited the liner in recognition of the ship's invaluable service in time of war. A small reception and luncheon were arranged in the converted children's playroom on the Upper Promenade Deck.

Soon afterward, the ship had her closest call in wartime. On Christmas Day 1944, when just off Halifax, she was warned of possible attack from a nearby U-boat. There was no mistake. Escorting destroyers dropped depth bombs. An underwater explosion followed and wreckage, oil and German books rose to the surface. The danger had been removed and the *Nieuw Amsterdam*, with just under 7,000 aboard, sailed off safely.

Other Holland America passenger ships were also part of many heroic voyages, escapes and rescues – and were very much part of the war at sea. 'We were caught in the colonial Dutch East Indies just as the invading Japanese were near,' remembered Hans de Jong. 'We had to pack quickly, but only some of our possessions, as time was running out. We were not sure where we were going or how. My family had come out from Holland in the 1920s and lived in the tropical setting with only occasional trips home to Amsterdam on those long, month-long sea voyages in each direction. In the 1940s, ships were still the only way to travel. My father made arrangements for our family and some luggage to board the *Noordam*, then a brand-new Holland America Line passenger-cargo ship [with 160 passenger berths] and which had been detoured in the early days of the war from North Atlantic service between Rotterdam and New York to special, long voyages out to Java and back. She was a comfortable ship, not yet converted for wartime, and so we were very fortunate to have very nice passenger cabins. We were, of course, relieved to get away from Batavia [now Djakarta], but the voyage was still quite tense. We heard that there were enemy subs in the Indian Ocean and even as we rounded the South African Cape and then headed up along the lower Atlantic, clinging to the South American coast and finally reaching the safety of New York harbor. It was my first visit to America, to famous Manhattan, to a world that seemed safe and free. I shall never forget the Holland America Line and the crew of the *Noordam* for the care given to us on that long, uncertain, six-week voyage.'

Two other Holland America ships were among the Second World War's great maritime sagas. The 1939-built *Zaandam*, sister ship of the aforementioned *Noordam*, was torpedoed by a Nazi U-boat while sailing off Brazil in November 1942. Sadly, the 10,700-ton ship sank within ten minutes, taking most of the passengers and crew to the bottom with her. Of the survivors, three drifted helplessly in a lifeboat, and without proper water and food, before being rescued eighty-two days later. Their period of endurance and survival remains the greatest on record. A close sister ship, the 12,000-ton *Westerdam*, would be sunk no less than three times during the war, but then, in extraordinary effort, revived and restored. A brand-new, still-incomplete passenger-cargo liner, intended for Rotterdam-North American West Coast service, she was sunk first in August 1942, during an Allied air raid on Nazi-occupied Rotterdam and its environs. The Nazis had her raised and sent off for repairs. In September 1944, the slowly retreating Nazi armies now planned a reverse in thinking. While they intended to deliberately sink her themselves as a harbor blockade, the Dutch Underground, the Resistance Forces, did the job first, but in a far less obstructive location. The Nazi high command was furious. They ordered that the 516-foot-long ship be raised and then re-sunk as a blockade. But again, the underground forces struck and so sank the ship again, a third time. The 134-passenger *Westerdam* was salvaged in September 1945, however, soon after the war in Europe ended, and was completely repaired. She was sailing to America by the late spring of 1946, in fact Holland America's first postwar luxury ship.

When Nazi Germany collapsed in May 1945, the *Nieuw Amsterdam* was, in fact, in the Mediterranean bound for Australia via the Suez. She was carrying homebound Aussie troops while her subsequent homebound voyage represented yet another political urgency: the evacuation of troubled Indonesia, the former colonial Dutch East Indies. The late Captain Kornelius van Herk recalled Christmas Day in 1945. 'We were at Port Said in the *Volendam* just as the *Nieuw Amsterdam* steamed past, loaded with more evacuees from Java.'

Anna Kruit lived in Holland during the war. 'Toward the end of the war in Europe, in 1944-45, things had actually gotten very sparse in Holland. It was our worst period actually. There was no food, little power – but just darkness and destruction. We were hopeful, however. We would soon rebuild and repair and start new lives. I especially remember bicycling to Rotterdam harbor in April 1946. The battle-scarred, rusting *Nieuw Amsterdam* was returning to her homeport for the first time since 1939, when the war in Europe started. I remember the newspaper stories of her being launched back in 1937 and being named by Queen Wilhelmina. Known for her size and luxuries, and because she was built completely in a Dutch shipyard using Dutch workers, the ship had a special place in many Dutch hearts. We were very, very proud of her. More than any other ship of that time, she was "Holland afloat". So on that spring day in 1946, there was a huge welcome in the harbor – people lining the shores, tooting tugs, waving flags, smiles and tears. The sounds of the horns and whistles was like a concert. We felt cheerful, hopeful, free. The sight of that great ship, the pride of the Dutch fleet and with her two smokestacks specially repainted in Holland America Line's yellow, green and white, was so moving. That ship symbolized more than anything else, the rebirth of postwar Holland. They called her "the Darling of the Dutch". Yes, she was our darling!'

Bill Seabrook, onetime public relations director of Holland America Line's New York office, wrote of the ship's return. 'The proud veteran returned to her home port on April 10th 1946, after an absence of six years and seven months. The date marked the ninth anniversary of her launching. For days, the city had been awaiting her return. She was their ship, their pride and an example of how Holland had contributed to victory. There were few persons in Rotterdam who had not had a part, or at least a very real interest, in her construction.'

Mr Seabrook continued, 'With a backdrop of black storm clouds, but with the sun shining directly upon her, she slowly proceeded up the Waterway. Everything that could float was out that day, clustering around the rust-streaked hull. Children lined the banks waving the Dutch tricolor. Onboard a welcoming launch, an ordinarily sophisticated newspaperman was seen to clasp his hands and shout, "the Darling of the Dutch!" Few ships ever received such an ovation.'

By the time the *Nieuw Amsterdam* was decommissioned from war duties at Rotterdam in April 1946, she had established a most heroic record: transporting 378,361 personnel during forty-four separate voyages for an average of 8,599 persons per sailing! Her travels were equivalent to nearly twenty-one times around the earth.

It cost 12,000,000 guilders to restore the *Nieuw Amsterdam* during her postwar refit (or just over 1,000,000 guilders less than she cost to build). Alone, the first fifteen weeks were needed just to remove the military fittings: the guns and hammocks, the standees and artillery. Then, as the actual restoration began, the 2,000 tons of original furniture was brought by freighter from San Francisco. Subsequently, over 3,000 chairs and 500 tables had to be send to their original makers. All of the ship's electrical wiring was replaced (itself, a stupendous task), all of the wood planed down to half the original thickness (to remove the thousands of deeply carved GI and other military initials), 12,000 square feet of glass renewed, 2,200 portholes replaced and the entire brasswork reburnished.

Holland America was indeed rethinking its place in the future of the reviving North Atlantic passenger trade. According to Italian ocean liner author and historian Maurizio Eliseo, in 1946, the company was considering buying the otherwise burnt-out hull of the 48,500-ton *Conte di Savoia*, the great pre-war Italian trans-Atlantic liner. With her engines basically intact, the thoughts were to rebuild the liner as a companion to the *Nieuw Amsterdam*. Shortage of money in those first postwar years as well as the great extent of the task shelved the idea in the end. Furthermore, during her refit and restoration, Holland America considered for a time extensively modernizing the *Nieuw Amsterdam*. Generally, the plan was to eliminate one funnel (the second was a dummy) and restyle her with a single mast and therefore much more contemporary look. But this idea was also abandoned.

At the very end, the *Nieuw Amsterdam* took a turn in the big King George V Graving Dock at Southampton, England, for the very final fitting-out.

Opposite page, Above left: Hoboken in the fall of 1939: the *Westernland* (left), the *Nieuw Amsterdam* (center) and the *Veendam* (right). (Steamship Historical Society of America)

Above right: Outbound on a Caribbean cruise from New York in the fall of 1939. This view is from the upper deck of a Lackawanna Railroad ferry in New York harbor. (Author's Collection)

Bottom left: The *Statendaam* III burns in Rotterdam harbor on 11 May 1940. (J&C McCutcheon Collection)

Bottom right: Off to war – troops fill the outer decks of the *Nieuw Amsterdam* seen here at Halifax. (Vincent Messina Collection)

Arriving home from a Caribbean cruise, the *Nieuw Amsterdam* wears neutrality markings in this view from the fall of 1939. (Albert Wilhelmi Collection)

Above left: At high speed at sea during the Second World War. (Holland America Line)

Above right: Cramped quarters – troop bunks aboard the *Nieuw Amsterdam*. (Vincent Messina Collection)

Below left: Triumph: the *Nieuw Amsterdam* returns to Rotterdam in April 1946, her first call at her homeport since September 1939. She has been dubbed 'the Darling of the Dutch'. (Vincent Messina Collection)

Below right: Restoration: the refit of the first-class Dining Room in 1947. (Vincent Messina Collection)

V

PEACETIME AND PROSPERITY: GRAND TIMES ON THE ATLANTIC

When the *Nieuw Amsterdam* resumed commercial sailings in October 1947, she was again the magnificent and very comfortable ship she was originally intended to be. More praises came her way as did a loyal relationship with yet another generation of sea travelers. Well-known figures often sailed in her: Albert Schweitzer, Rita Hayworth, Spencer Tracey, Jane Russell, Katharine Hepburn and the King of Belgium.

After the Second World War, Holland America resumed its celebrated service between Hoboken and northern Europe, and on cruises in winter. There was the *Nieuw Amsterdam, Veendam, Volendam, Westerdam* and *Noordam*, and beginning in 1951-52, the sisters *Ryndam* and *Maasdam*, which were 15,000-ton, 875-passenger luxury liners, but which offered very affordable passages: $20 per person per day in tourist class. On such comfortable, well-run ships, this was not just innovative, but revolutionary. Tourist-class passengers had 90 per cent of the ship's spaces (there were only thirty-nine berths in clubby, top-deck first class) and these included pleasant lounges, a movie theatre and even an outdoor swimming pool. Never before had tourist-class passengers been accorded such amenities, comfort, modern style.

The 15,000-ton *Veendam* was restored for regular commercial service after falling into Nazi hands during the Second World War. Captain Frederick van Driel was a young seaman aboard the *Veendam* when, in October 1948, she made Holland America's first tropical cruise to the Caribbean following the war. 'We did not have air-conditioning back then and especially on an older ship like the *Veendam*,' he remembered. 'To make matters worse, she had very dark, very cluttered, very heavy décor.

Although everyone dressed, often in formal attire, in those days, the ship was like a floating steam bath. Younger passengers actually slept on deck in the Caribbean and, during the day, we erected a canvas tank and filled it with seawater, and so this served as a swimming pool and some relief. Even later, in the 1950s, I remember being aboard the *Nieuw Amsterdam* in ports such as Havana, Kingston and Port au Prince, and the ship was sweltering. She had only very limited air-conditioning in some public areas, but the cabins and corridors were very warm. Longtime passengers knew well the benefits of an outside cabin with a porthole.'

Those first, post-Second World War cruises brought an added notation to Holland America's rich history. While the ship's purser was previously responsible for passenger entertainment, amusement and diversion, a new, separate position was created aboard the *Nieuw Amsterdam* and *Veendam* during those winter, escape-to-the-sun cruises in the late 1940s. The term 'cruise director' was invented and is in use on all cruise ships today. Years later, in the early 1970s, the chief purser's role was renamed to suit the new age of these floating resorts. This post was reinvented as the 'hotel manager' aboard Holland America liners. Also, at the same time, Holland America initiated a 'no tipping' policy as well as a 'cashless' system onboard their by then blue-hulled liners.

Captain Kornelius van Herk served aboard the *Nieuw Amsterdam* on a number of occasions, beginning in the 1950s, and remembered her as 'a good sea ship, strong and solid. However, in heavy weather, we always had to reduce her speed very quickly. Once, the bridge windows were smashed during a North Atlantic storm, while on another occasion, the window

of the chief officer's cabin was shattered. His cabin began to flood. Later, during the clean-up, crewmen found a huge piece of splintered glass in the chief's bedroom, a full room behind the area with the broken window. Also, we had to be very careful with the *Nieuw Amsterdam* when going full astern. The trembling was very bad. In fact, hundreds of light bulbs would have to be replaced afterward.'

Opposite: The First Class Dining Room. (J&C McCutcheon Collection)

Left: Back in business! The *Nieuw Amsterdam* in a post-Second World War postcard. (Author's Collection)

Nighttime at Rotterdam in the late 1940s. (Albert Wilhelmi Collection)

Right: American maritime artist Don Stoltenberg's commemorative poster art of the *Nieuw Amsterdam*. (Don Stoltenberg Collection)

Below: A postcard rendition of the liner in the 1950s. (Albert Wilhelmi Collection)

Above: Passing through the Panama Canal on her Around South America cruise. (Richard Faber Collection)

Left: Berthed at Boston's Commonwealth Pier in the 1950s. (Richard Faber Collection)

Right: Docked at Rio de Janeiro. (Albert Wilhelmi Collection)

Above left: Outbound from Rotterdam in the 1950s. (Albert Wilhelmi Collection)

Above right: Dressed in flags: another view from the Panama Canal. (Albert Wilhelmi Collection)

Left: The *Nieuw Amsterdam* at Cristobal, Panama, with the United Fruit passenger-cargo ship *Jamaica* on the right. (Albert Wilhelmi Collection)

Right: Another view from Cristobal during the winter cruise season – the *Nieuw Amsterdam* is in center and the *Ile de France* is to the right. A Royal Netherlands Steamship Co. cargo vessel is on the left. (Albert Wilhelmi

A busy day at the Wilton-Fijenoord Shipyard at Schiedam in the 1950s. Along with other vessels, the passenger-cargo liner *Diemerdyk* of Holland America is on the far left while the *Maasdam* and then the *Nieuw Amsterdam* are in the center. (Albert Wilhelmi Collection)

Above left: The *Nieuw Amsterdam* departs from the Wilhelminakade with the *Ryndam* just behind. (Albert Wilhelmi Collection)

Above right: The *Nieuw Amsterdam* berthed at the Wilhelminakade in Rotterdam. (Vincent Messina Collection)

Left: An aerial view of a sailing from Le Havre. (Holland America Line)

Above left: The *Nieuw Amsterdam* passes the new flagship *Rotterdam* in mid-Atlantic. (Holland America Line)

Above right: The *Nieuw Amsterdam* departing from New York's Pier 90, with the *Bremen* berthed on the right. (Vincent Messina Collection)

Right: The *Nieuw Amsterdam* and *Rotterdam* exchanging berths at Hoboken in 1959. (Holland America Line)

Above: On a few occasions, the *Nieuw Amsterdam* berthed along New York City's 'Lower Luxury Liner'. She is seen here, in an evening view, at Pier 92 in a view dated August 1969. (Author's Collection)

Left: The distinctive funnels by night. (Author's Collection)

Above left: Outbound in the New Waterway. (Vincent Messina Collection)

Above right: The funnels as seen at New York. (Author's Collection)

Right: At anchor at St Thomas in the Caribbean. (Holland America Line)

Above: At anchor in Norway's Geirangerfjord. (Vincent Messina Collection)

Left: An evocative brochure cover from the 1950s. (Author's Collection)

Below: Southampton, 19 June 1968. (J&C McCutcheon Collection)

VI

THE HAL FLEET: 'IT IS GOOD TO BE ON A WELL-RUN SHIP'

The late C. M. Squarey, a noted connoisseur of passenger ships, especially in the late 1940s and through the 1950s, was delighted with the *Nieuw Amsterdam*. 'I can't resist saying,' in his book of observations, appraisals and recollections of 1955, 'that if ships were ever to have slogans of their own, one for the *Nieuw Amsterdam* might run, "It's even better still to be on a very well-run ship."'

He continued in his writings dated June 1949, after having made a short, but important round voyage from Southampton to Rotterdam and then return to Southampton. 'This ship, of nearly 37,000 tons, is generally conceded to be of beautiful proportions – indeed, she has lovely lines. But if there are any shipping people who have not seen the interior layout of this ship, it would not be a waste of time to do so.'

Mr Squarey was back aboard the *Nieuw Amsterdam* in October 1951 and wrote, 'She is a grand and very well-run ship. When I have to write about her again, I would not withdraw a word of the complimentary things I have said in the past.'

A onetime master of New York harbor's Staten Island ferries as well as a seafarer and enthusiastic ship collector, Captain Ed Squire recalled seeing the *Nieuw Amsterdam* during the 1950s. 'I feel the *Nieuw Amsterdam* was somewhat nicer than the comparably-sized *Mauretania* [1939] yet on equal par with the *America* [1940]. *The Ile of France*, also of similar size, was to me in a class by herself. While the *Ile* had been greatly rebuilt after the Second World War with two instead of three funnels, the *Nieuw Amsterdam* retained most of her original interiors and exterior structure as did both the *Mauretania* and *America*. Throughout her life, the *Nieuw Amsterdam*

was one of the most magnificent ships of her time, both in size, design and interior beauty. I remember seeing this beautiful vessel in the early 1950s at Holland America's Hoboken pier. My parents and I watched her sail for Europe. We stood on the very docks where the great film *On the Waterfront* had just been filmed. To me, the *Nieuw Amsterdam* was the "little" *Queen Elizabeth* just as I felt the *Queen of Bermuda* was "little" *Queen Mary*. Several years later, while watching from Grace Line's Pier 57 in Manhattan and directly across from Hoboken, I watched intently as the *Nieuw Amsterdam* and the *Rotterdam* were shifting berths in 1959. The *Nieuw Amsterdam* looked the classic liner with her recently repainted gray hull. I liked the *Nieuw Amsterdam* more than the new *Rotterdam*. Later, in the 1960s, I was invited aboard the *Nieuw Amsterdam* after Holland America Line moved to new Pier 40 in Manhattan. I really admired the interiors, public rooms, dining rooms and passenger staterooms. She impressed me as a very beautiful and a very comfortable liner. Also, the *Nieuw Amsterdam*'s crew and staff always showed the most wonderful Dutch hospitality. On both counts, the *Nieuw Amsterdam* lived up to her Dutch tradition as the "Darling of the Dutch" and that "it was good to be on a well-run ship".'

First-class ocean liner collector Der Scutt made his very first voyage on the Dutch flagship. He remembered, 'The *Nieuw Amsterdam* was the first ship I ever made crossing onboard. It was especially awesome because I was completely naïve about ships and had only left my family's farm in eastern Pennsylvania on two occasions – once on a day trip to Philadelphia and once on a class trip to New York City. I was about to enter the World on this shipboard sailing experience.

'However, being a young architect at age nineteen, I was particularly impressed with just seeing the *Nieuw Amsterdam* for the first time. Her stately forms, magnificent composition of elements and tailored proportions signaled a vessel of impeccable beauty. Berthed in Hoboken, the crowded waterfront community just across from Manhattan and amidst the hustle and bustle of cargo handing and passenger embarkations, the ship stood out with unsurpassed majesty. I didn't know anything about ocean liners, but my sensitivity for design idealism established an immediate logic of superb marine composition.'

In the booming 1950s on the North Atlantic, Holland America offered frequent sailings. A sample schedule for May 1957 included these sailings eastbound from New York:

Sat May 4th	*Westerdam*
Wed May 8th	*Maasdam*
Fri May 10th	*Nieuw Amsterdam*
Fri May 17th	*Statendam*
Sat May 18th	*Noordam*
Wed May 29th	*Ryndam*
Fri May 31st	*Nieuw Amsterdam*

Peak summer season fares on the *Nieuw Amsterdam* were posted from $300 in first class, from $230 in cabin class and from $190 in tourist class.

By the late 1950s, Holland America returned to its full stride in providing sun-seeking, off-season, winter cruises. The *Nieuw Amsterdam* departed, for example, for fourteen days to the Caribbean with rates from $435, while the brand-new *Statendam* cruised the Mediterranean for thirty-nine days with fares from $910. A short, summer cruise to Bermuda on the *Maasdam* was priced from $145.

The 1961-62 fall/winter/spring cruise schedule from New York included:

Statendam	Nov 8th	12 days	Caribbean
Statendam	Nov 20th	14 days	Caribbean
Nieuw Amsterdam	Dec 6th	12 ½ days	Caribbean
Rotterdam	Dec 20th	15 days	Caribbean
Nieuw Amsterdam	Dec 21st	12 days	Caribbean
Maasdam	Dec 23rd	11 days	Caribbean
Nieuw Amsterdam	Jan 3rd	11 ½ days	Caribbean
Rotterdam	Jan 6th	15 days	Caribbean
Nieuw Amsterdam	Jan 17th	14 days	Caribbean
Statendam	Jan 24th	16 days	Caribbean
Rotterdam	Jan 25th	80 days	Around the World
Nieuw Amsterdam	Feb 3rd	15 days	Caribbean
Statendam	Feb 11th	14 days	Caribbean
Nieuw Amsterdam	Feb 20th	14 days	Caribbean
Statendam	Feb 28th	12 days	Caribbean
Nieuw Amsterdam	Mar 7th	11 days	Caribbean
Statendam	Mar 13th	9 ½ days	Caribbean
Nieuw Amsterdam	Mar 20th	13 ½ days	Caribbean
Statendam	Mar 26th	12 days	Caribbean
Nieuw Amsterdam	Apr 6th	9 days	Caribbean
Nieuw Amsterdam	Apr 16th	5 ½ days	Bermuda
Maasdam	May 27th	10 days	Caribbean

On the Atlantic and also for winter cruises, the *Nieuw Amsterdam* was often booked to capacity. Her popularity and acclaim did not diminish with age. Instead, it actually grew further. Increasingly, her period interiors became something akin to a 'floating grand hotel'. There were still many travelers who yearned for the 'good old days'. To them, a ship such as the *Nieuw Amsterdam* was often their choice.

The 1950s North Atlantic was, in many ways, dominated by the four largest liners of the day: the *Queen Mary* and *Queen Elizabeth*, the brand-new *United States*, which was also the fastest liner afloat, and the *Liberté* of the French Line. The *Nieuw Amsterdam*, while the Dutch flagship, was in fact more in the intermediate class of Atlantic liners, those between 30-50,000 tons. She had several close peers. 'The *Nieuw Amsterdam* was more of a "first-class liner" in my opinion than the second *Mauretania*, which was intended to be a "relief ship" for the mighty Queens,' noted ocean liner enthusiast Pine Hodges. 'Otherwise, the *America* was a smaller vessel, and most likely more "Spartan" in terms of her interior appointments. Actually, the *Ile de France* was her closest rival in terms of size, décor and decoration, and fame. The *Nieuw Amsterdam* was definitely a prettier ship as built, while the *Ile de France* looked more like a "Ship of State" only following her 1949 refit, in which her hull line was lowered a full deck and two larger, wider funnels replaced the original three. The *Nieuw Amsterdam* was pure beauty. Unlike the *Ile*, she needed no such "Trompe Doeil", as she had impressive sheer as built and thus she needed no extra embellishment. Indeed, the *Nieuw Amsterdam* retained her good looks from start to finish.'

The new 24,000-ton *Statendam* – with a new configuration of a mere eighty-four in upper-deck first class and 867 in very comfortable tourist class – first arrived in February 1957. She was a great success, following in the wake of the highly successful, tourist-class-dominated sisters *Ryndam* and *Maasdam* of 1951-52. But bigger and grander still, the 38,000-ton *Rotterdam* was introduced in September 1959. She had fine lounges and salons, a twin-level theater, two sumptuous dining rooms, an indoor as well as outdoor pool, and a private bathroom in every cabin.

The new Dutch liners were in some contrast, however. Albert Wilhelmi, a devoted passenger-ship traveler and collector, traveled to Europe in 1964. 'I would have liked to have sailed on the *Nieuw Amsterdam*, but her tourist class did not compare to those aboard the new *Statendam* and *Rotterdam*. There were private facilities in the tourist-class cabins on the newer ships, for example. So, with some regret having never sailed on the grand *Nieuw Amsterdam*, we selected the *Rotterdam* for the trip over and then home on the *Statendam*.'

It wasn't all high luxury, however, aboard Dutch passenger ships sailing the North Atlantic. Holland America also operated low-fare ships for students, their teachers and chaperones, and immigrants. Three of them were converted Second World War troop transports, members of the mass-produced Victory Ships. They were named for constellations – *Groote Beer* (Great Bear), *Waterman* (Aquarius) and *Zuiderkruis* (Southern Cross). Smallish ships of just over 9,000 tons, but able to carry as many as 800 passengers, all in budget, rather austere tourist class, they were never intended for luxury service. They offered bargain passages – $140 for the nine-day trip from New York to Rotterdam in 1960, for example. Other student and low-fare ships that sailed for Holland America in the 1950s and 1960s included the *Sibajak*, *Seven Seas*, *Johan van Oldenbarnevelt* and, on class-divided around-the-world voyages, two noted Dutch liners of the time, the *Willem Ruys* and the *Oranje*.

Captain Hans van Biljouw remembered his service with the great Holland America Line and its trans-Atlantic liners. 'The job of captain was quite divine. It was a world almost without boundaries, a world of power, challenge, romance and elegance. It is a great personal adventure and a distinct way of life. Sailing for the Holland America Line was both a pleasure and a privilege. We had beautiful ships, excellent crew members and an enormous variety of itineraries – crossings as well as cruises. I well remember spending some years, beginning in 1964, on the flagship *Rotterdam*, then the flagship of the entire Dutch merchant marine. We were still running crossings then, from April through October, between Rotterdam, Le Havre, Southampton and New York, and these were fully booked. The ship was divided by special panels in the corridors and on the stairwells that separated first class and tourist class [the *Rotterdam* carried

401 passengers in first class and 1,055 in tourist]. Today, if we closed such panels, which divided the ship, there would be great confusion. But passengers were accustomed to class-divided ships back then.'

The *Nieuw Amsterdam* was given three major facelifts, to ensure her competitiveness and, on at least one occasion, to ensure her life. In the winter of 1956/57, during an extended overhaul, her accommodation was upgraded, full air-conditioning was added and the hull repainted in dove gray (replacing the previous black and considered better for heart resistance during winter cruises in the tropics). In the winter refit of 1961/62, the liner was restyled as a first- and tourist-class ship with the original cabin class being eliminated. Her berthing arrangements actually became more flexible, according to demand: either 691 in first class and 583 in tourist or 301 first and 972 tourist.

But the third and most critical refit came in 1967. In that summer, the *Nieuw Amsterdam* had a severe mechanical breakdown, such that her sailings had to be cancelled and her passengers transferred to other ships. 'She was getting old, wearing out and had become a ship of many Band-Aids,' remembered the late Cees Tensen, a former vice president with Holland America Line. Rumors flew that the twenty-nine-year-old liner – "the Dutchman's favorite", as she was further nicknamed – would be scrapped. Further rumors indicated that Holland America was bidding to buy the two-year-old, 39,000-ton *Oceanic* from the Home Lines as an immediate replacement. But Holland America directors conferred with shipyard engineers. She would be repaired and saved!

Captain van Herk remembered this tense period: 'The management definitely wanted to save her. The shipyard agreed that she could be saved, but that new, expensive boilers were needed. Then, Holland America was very lucky. They were able to buy appropriate secondhand boilers from a retired US Navy cruiser in California. These were brought to Holland in the company's *Moerdyk* and delivered directly to the Wilton-Fijenoord Shipyard at Schiedam, where the twenty-nine-year-old liner was waiting. The Wilton people had already burned a huge opening in the side of the *Nieuw Amsterdam* and then removed the old, worn-out boilers. The new 'secondhand' boilers were installed in rather record time and were, in fact, considerable improvements. The ship actually had one boiler less than before, and the units were smaller and much lighter. In fact, we needed extra ballast afterwards. The "transplant" proved to be very efficient and good, rendering the same service as before.'

Over the years, the *Nieuw Amsterdam* was not without her occasional mishaps. On January 4th 1965, while returning from her annual Christmas Caribbean cruise, she had a collision in Lower New York Bay, in the early morning hours, with an unlit railway barge. She briefly stopped and then proceeded to her berth at Pier 40 in Manhattan. Divers inspected the damage, which was found to be slight, and she sailed on schedule, on the 7th, for her next cruise.

On another occasion, Captain van Herk was aboard during an otherwise quiet overnight stay, docked on the north side of Pier 40. 'Suddenly, a tremendous shock rocked the empty ship. It was later discovered that a fully loaded railroad carfloat was coming down the Hudson River and hit the stern. The carfloat swung over to the west side of Pier 40. Some stern frames on the *Nieuw Amsterdam* were dented as a result.' On still another occasion, she hit a pierside crane at the Wilhelminakade in Rotterdam. The aft tug that was used in the docking was not powerful enough and so the liner suddenly shifted in her own wake.

Above: An aerial view of the Wilhelminakade dated 1951. The *Nieuw Amsterdam* is on the lower left, the *Westerdam* on the right and *Volendam* is laid-up in the background. (Gillespie-Faber Collection)

Right: Departing from Rotterdam. (Richard Faber Collection)

Above left: An outbound voyage from her homeport. (Albert Wilhelmi Collection)

Above right: The *Nieuw Amsterdam* passing the Hook of Holland. (Richard Faber Collection)

Below left: The second funnel was a dummy, as evidenced in this view. (Richard Faber Collection)

Below right: The *Nieuw Amsterdam* being towed in the New Waterway. (Richard Faber Collection)

Above left: Busy day at the Wilhelminakade in the 1950s: the *Maasdam* (top), the *Nieuw Amsterdam* (center) and the *Zuiderkruis* (lower right). (Gillespie-Faber Collection)

Above right: A postcard view of the *Nieuw Amsterdam* from the 1950s. (Albert Wilhelmi Collection)

Left: A colorful view of the *Nieuw Amsterdam* by Dutch artist Robert Murk). (Albert Wilhelmi Collection)

Above : A festive Holland America departure scene. (Albert Wilhelmi Collection)

Left: A superb poster of the *Nieuw Amsterdam* first created in 1953. (Albert Wilhelmi Collection)

Above left: A Moran tug helps berth the *Nieuw Amsterdam* at Hoboken in this 1955 photo. (Moran Towing & Transportation Co.)

Above right: No fewer than five Moran tugs assist in this afternoon docking in 1949 at Hoboken as the flag-bedecked *Nieuw Amsterdam* returns from a Caribbean cruise. (Moran Towing & Transportation Co.)

Below left: A glorious stern view of the *Nieuw Amsterdam* as she enters the slip at the 5th Street pier. The Egyptian combination passenger-cargo liner *Mohammed Ali El Kebir* is to the left, the *Noordam* on the right. (Moran Towing & Transportation Co.)

Below right: An aerial view of the Hoboken piers in October 1948. The *Nieuw Amsterdam* is in center position. (Hoboken Historical Museum)

Above left: The *Nieuw Amsterdam* seen here in mid-Hudson in the 1950s. (Moran Towing & Transportation Co.)

Above right: The late Frank Braynard was a superb marine artist. He sketched and drew countless ships, including this view of the *Nieuw Amsterdam* passing the Lower Manhattan skyline. The sketch was made in the early 1980s for the *Fifty Famous Liners* series. (Captain James McNamara Collection)

Right: Anchored at Santos, Brazil, during her 1953 Carnival in Rio cruise. (Laire Jose Giraud)

Above left: Outbound from New York late on a Friday afternoon. (Port Authority of New York & New Jersey)

Above right: Winter overhaul: the *Nieuw Amsterdam* is in dry dock at the Wilton-Fijenoord shipyard at Schiedam. The *Indrapoera* of Royal Rotterdam Lloyd is on the lower left and, at top, the immigrant ships *Goya*, Norwegian owned (left), and the *Fairsea*, Sitmar Line (right). (Albert Wilhelmi Collection)

Left: The Grand Hall was highlighted by the massive cast-aluminum bas-relief suspended from the ceiling. (Vincent Messina Collection)

Above left: Another view of the Grand Hall, but as seen after the Second World War. Note the orchestra on the upper-level gallery. (Vincent Messina Collection)

Above right: Another view of the Grand Hall. (Albert Wilhelmi Collection)

Right: The first-class Smoking Room was highlighted by its fine walnut paneling. (Albert Wilhelmi Collection)

Above left: The exquisite ebony and bronze stairway in first class in which art and function have been ideally coupled. (Albert Wilhelmi Collection)

Above right: The cozy Jungle Bar. (Albert Wilhelmi Collection)

Left: The stunning Champlain Dining Room with Moroccan leather ceilings and Murano chandeliers. (Albert Wilhelmi Collection)

Above left: A night view of the Champlain Dining Room. (Vincent Messina Collection)

Above right: The golden, padded ceiling, tinted mirrors and soft, diffused lighting lend to a quiet, almost serene atmosphere for fine dining onboard the *Nieuw Amsterdam.* (Vincent Messina Collection)

Right: The Champlain Dining Room was fed by escalators from the kitchens, the only ones of their type on a liner in the late 1940s. (Vincent Messina Collection)

Above left: The impressive silver model of Henry Hudson's *Half Moon* sat at the base of the grand staircase. (Vincent Messina Collection)

Above right: Attention to detail: the mermaid door handles at the entrance to the Smoking Room bar. (Vincent Messina Collection)

Right: The panel of the Four Seasons in the grand lobby of the *Nieuw Amsterdam*. (Vincent Messina Collection)

Above left: A wood panel depicting the history of Dutch seafaring. (Vincent Messina Collection)

Above right: Another view of the inviting Smoking Room. (Vincent Messina Collection)

Right: The shopping arcade. (Vincent Messina Collection)

Above left: All regular first-class cabins had private bathroom facilities. (Vincent Messina Collection)

Above right: The Gala Buffet in the Grand Hall during a winter cruise in the 1960s. (Holland America Line)

Left: The classic beauty of the *Nieuw Amsterdam* is quite clear in this view of the ship in the New Waterway. (Albert Wilhelmi Collection)

Fleetmates: the *Statendam* (left) and the *Nieuw Amsterdam* together at the Wilhelminakade. (Gillespie-Faber Collection)

Silhouetted in late afternoon light, another view of the *Nieuw Amsterdam* in the New Waterway. (Richard Faber Collection)

The *Nieuw Amsterdam* arriving at Hoboken from a winter Caribbean cruise in a scene dated January 1959. (Author's Collection)

Above left: Three Moran tugs are at the bow section as the *Nieuw Amsterdam* docks. (Author's Collection)

Above right: The Dutch hospital ship *Henry Dunant* passes the *Nieuw Amsterdam* at Rotterdam. (Albert Wilhelmi Collection)

Left: Fueling the great liner in Rotterdam. (Author's Collection)

Above left: A well-framed view of the *Nieuw Amsterdam* and *Rotterdam*. (Author's Collection)

Above right: Outbound at Rotterdam. (Albert Wilhelmi Collection)

Right: Another splendid view of one of the most beautiful liners of the twentieth century. (Albert Wilhelmi Collection)

Above left: The busy port of Rotterdam. (Author's Collection)

Above right: Together at the Wilton-Fijenoord Shipyard at Schiedam – the *Nieuw Amsterdam* on the left, the *Rotterdam* on the right. (Albert Wilhelmi Collection)

Below left: A splendid aerial view: returning from a cruise and inbound at New York. (Flying Camera Inc.)

Below right: Outbound in New York's Lower Bay. (Albert Wilhelmi Collection)

Above left: Swapping berths at Hoboken: the *Nieuw Amsterdam* and *Rotterdam* exchange use of the 5th Street pier in Hoboken in this view dated December 1959. (Flying Camera Inc.)

Above right: Holland America Line's new Pier 40 opened in March 1962. In this scene, dated April 23rd 1963, the *Nieuw Amsterdam* is on the left, the *Westerdam* is at the outer berth and the *Oranje* is on the right. (Holland America Line)

Right: Still incomplete, Pier 40 is behind the outbound *Nieuw Amsterdam* in this view from the winter of 1962. (Albert Wilhelmi Collection)

Above: A spectacular view from the forward mast as the ship is underway. (Holland America Line)

Left: The *Nieuw Amsterdam* at the Wilton-Fijenoord shipyard. (Wilton-Fijenoord B. V.)

Above: Arriving at New York with the Statue of Liberty in the background. (Holland America Line)

Right: Classic liners: the *Nieuw Amsterdam* and *Rotterdam* together at the Wilhelminakade in the twilight of the Atlantic liner trade. (Holland America Line)

Left: The *Rotterdam*'s maiden departure from Southampton, September 4, 1959. (J&C McCutcheon Collection)

Below, left: Italy's *Michelangelo* and the *Nieuw Amsterdam* at New York in August 1969. (Vincent Messina Collection).

Below, right: A nighttime view at Barbados dated 1969. (Vincent Messina Collection)

The *Veendam* berthed at Hoboken in 1952. (Author's Collection)

Above: The last remains of the Holland America Line terminal at Hoboken in a view dated March 1983. (Author's Collection)

Left: A brochure cover from the 1960s. (Vincent Messina Collection)

Above left: The splendid *Rotterdam* sailing off Capetown during a world cruise. (Holland America Line)

Above right: The *Statendam* arriving in New York harbor in 1957. (Holland America Line)

Left: The handsome *Maasdam* departing from the Wilhelminakade in the early 1950s. (Holland America Line)

VII

TWILIGHT AND THEN SUNSET IN THE EAST

In March 1957, when the *Nieuw Amsterdam* returned to New York following her winter overhaul, there was a noticeable change – she was repainted with a gray hull. But other, far greater changes were ahead. In October 1958, the first commercial passenger jets flew the Atlantic. The ocean liner business would never again be the same. A huge success with the appeal of great speed, the airlines firmly secured two-thirds of all trans-ocean traffic within as little as six months. By 1963, aircraft had as much as 95 per cent of all travelers. Holland America, like all other Atlantic shipping lines, was in ways slow to grasp this transition.

There was fleet reshuffling by the 1960s, varied attempts to maintain profitability within the passenger fleet. The *Ryndam* was sent off on a new Rotterdam-Montreal service beginning in 1960, the *Maasdam* began extended trans-Atlantic service that included Bremerhaven commencing in 1963 and the latter ship inaugurated winter service to Australia and around the world in 1965. But it was all becoming more and more of a struggle. The airlines were showing their strength and might. In 1966, the nine-year-old *Statendam* was reassigned to full-time cruising. That same year, the *Ryndam* was placed in mostly student service, sailing for the affiliated Europe-Canada Line. In 1968, the *Maasdam* was sold off, becoming the Polish *Stefan Batory*. A year later, the *Rotterdam* began being used as a full-time cruise ship. On the Atlantic, the aged *Nieuw Amsterdam* was left to sail singlehandedly. For extra revenue and passenger appeal, her westbound sailings to New York often included a stop at Halifax for the ease of Canada-bound passengers. Her cruising schedule now also included the occasional summer trips from Rotterdam,

such as a scenic voyage to the Norwegian fjords. But with her age, she was also becoming an increasingly expensive ship to operate.

The trans-Atlantic liner trade was changing quickly, its decline rapid and dramatic. The likes of the *Queen Mary* and *Queen Elizabeth*, long since operating in the red, were withdrawn in 1967-68. The *United States* followed in 1969 and finally the comparatively new *France* was decommissioned in 1974, after only twelve years of service. The brand-new *Queen Elizabeth 2* was first commissioned, however, in 1969. Said to be the last Atlantic liner, she was, from the start, facing an uncertain future. Amidst a storm of change and uncertainty, Holland America had to rethink its future. Quite simply, the veteran *Nieuw Amsterdam* was no longer a viable economic proposition.

That grand old ship was, quite ironically, used to close out the company's 100-year-old trans-Atlantic passenger service in September 1971. The jet had finally won. The *Nieuw Amsterdam* – 'the grand old lady' as some called her – was assigned to join the *Rotterdam*, *Statendam* and other Holland America liners in year-round cruise service from US ports. She would never again visit Holland.

The late Vincent Messina, a great fan of Holland America and in particular of the grand old *Nieuw Amsterdam*, remained loyal to the ship to her very last sailings. He was aboard several Caribbean cruises in her in the early 1970s. 'She was by then a grand hangover from the past – with woods, brass, two-deck-high lounges – that seemed a world apart from the new, emerging generation of sleek, white-hulled cruise ships. The new breed seemed to be all plastic, metallic and velours,' said Messina. 'Of course, there were fewer conveniences on a ship such as the *Nieuw Amsterdam*. There were still many cabins, for example, without private bathroom facilities. The rates, of course, reflected this: $350 per person for eleven days in the Caribbean without a private shower and toilet; $500 per person with private facilities [1971].

'The service was also of another age. It was strict French silver service,' added Messina. 'There were trays for meats, for example. On current ships, in this era of often hard economics, it's either full-plate service or quasi-plate service. It is less elegant, somewhat more like Horn & Hardart gone to sea. There was also less to do on ships like the *Nieuw Amsterdam*. There were far fewer of the elaborate entertainment programs now found on cruise liners. Most of the *Nieuw Amsterdam*'s passengers went for the time at sea, for the rest and relaxation. Cruising to them meant time at sea. Today, it is all fast paced, fly to the sun and eight ports in seven days. It seems to be time on the ship as a floating hotel and far more time in ports for the likes of shopping and swimming.'

Her final employment was a series of Caribbean cruises from Port Everglades, Florida. But in 1973, Holland America lost some $12.5 million on their passenger operations, caused mainly by the new, highly increased fuel oil costs. Rather quickly, the thirty-five-year-old *Nieuw Amsterdam* was selected for disposal. However, Captain van Herk felt that she still had yet another five years of life left. 'She was not worn out. She was still very well maintained. Instead, the problems were in the engine room mostly. It was pure slavery for those men down below, especially since we were now always in the Caribbean. The *Nieuw Amsterdam* did not have a good cooling system in her engine room. Furthermore, too many people were needed to keep her sailing. Her crew size was simply too large, especially in a time of trimming expenses. Nowadays [1982], aboard, say, the new Scandinavian cruise ships, the engine rooms are controlled from air-conditioned, glass-enclosed booths. They need a very small staff and are even closed down at night and operated completely from the bridge.'

Holland America Line itself released a farewell booklet commemorating the vintage ship. It read: 'The *Nieuw Amsterdam* was created for an era when "luxury liner" was not just a phrase, but a glorious reality. Although still a great and seaworthy vessel, she can no longer be operated economically in this hemisphere without sacrificing some of the standards that have contributed to her greatness in the past. Out of Holland America's sorrowful decision to retire this gracious ship in December 1973, comes a golden opportunity for you to recreate warm experiences on one of *Nieuw Amsterdam*'s retirement cruises. These final ten-day Caribbean cruises from Port Everglades represent the last chance for our passengers to return to an age when a voyage on the *Nieuw Amsterdam*

was one of life's most treasured experiences. You will relax once again in an atmosphere of absolute grandeur amid shimmering mirrors, gleaming bronze and brass, warm woods and rich textures. The *Nieuw Amsterdam* is a marine masterpiece of distinctive art, tasteful décor and extravagant use of space. She has been aptly called the "Versailles of vessels"!'

Vincent Messina was aboard her final cruise, scheduled just before the Christmas-New Year holidays. He recalled, 'The majority of the passengers on that final cruise were "old cruisers", loyalists to the ship and to the sea and to whom it didn't matter where they went. Among them was Mrs Elinora de Lara Kates, who was on her 219th voyage with Holland America. It was her sixtieth voyage in the *Nieuw Amsterdam*, which included the maiden voyage in May 1938. A special cocktail party was given in her honor and the invitations were printed in pink silk. At the gathering, she announced her wishes were to die on this beloved liner.'

Messina added, 'The last cruise was a pre-Christmas trip, which was usually the most difficult to book. It was always a weak seller. Thereafter, the annual Christmas trip from Port Everglades would be aboard the smaller *Statendam*. Some of the great treasures remained on the *Nieuw Amsterdam*, such as her mermaid door handles in the Smoking Room and the silver model of Henry Hudson's *Half Moon*. Months later, however, there were crates at New York, at Holland America's Pier 40, that were marked from the *Nieuw Amsterdam* and then bound for the Rotterdam home office. [The *Half Moon* model, for example, later found its way to the company's Seattle headquarters.]

'It was all very sad, and on the night before her last night at sea with passengers, the air-conditioning went out. However, everyone stayed in the lounge just the same to see the final variety performances. The ship became a steam bath. The band played 'Sentimental Journey' and everyone cried. She was indeed a very special ship with a very definite soul. In her final years, Holland America did an excellent job promoting the age of the ship: 'In this age of chrome and instant coffee, this is a ship of soaring ceilings and inlaid woods and ebony staircases. No, they don't make ships like this any more and it's a shame!'

The fate of the *Nieuw Amsterdam* fed many rumors. Of course, there was talk that she would go to a Greek cruise line for further trading. Others suggested that she should be made into a museum and hotel ship, especially at her former homeport of Rotterdam (Holland America liners had been re-registered at Curacao in the Dutch West Indies beginning in 1973). The most vivid yet least probable rumor, however, was that the ship would be bought by the City of Rotterdam, but to become a 'sex centre'. This tale continued that the City Fathers wanted to centralize its red light district, and concentrate it aboard the old *Nieuw Amsterdam*, which, in an extension of the rumor, would be docked permanently at the Parkhaven or even the rarely used Wilhelminakade, the former Holland America Line terminal. The company itself was particularly quiet during the time of these rumors. In reality, as good Dutch businessmen, they were simply waiting for the highest bidder.

In the end, she was sold, similar to so many other, older liners of the time, to a Taiwanese scrap metal firm. She fetched a price of nearly 13 million guilders – again the same price that she cost to build originally in 1937-38 and about the same as her post-Second World War restoration in 1946-47. So, after her final cruise to the Caribbean from Florida in December 1973, she sailed through the Panama Canal and then onward to Los Angeles to take on fuel and provisions for the slow and final crossing of the Pacific.

Captain James McNamara recalled that final voyage. 'A friend boarded the ship at Long Beach (Los Angeles), where she was bunkering. He was invited to lunch onboard the otherwise scrapyard-bound liner. But to his great surprise, he found that the large main dining room was still immaculate, completely in place and laid out with full china, cutlery and linens. He was given a full lunch. He was amazed at the overall condition of the ship. She was pristine, as if preparing for another cruise. When he asked one of the ship's officers, the response was: 'She will remain in perfect condition until handed over to the scrappers. After all, she is still a Holland America liner until then.'

Under the command of Captain R. ten Kate, the *Nieuw Amsterdam* almost reluctantly sailed eastward to Taiwan at a meek 12 knots. She carried a greatly reduced maintenance and operational crew of sixty.

She arrived at Kaohsiung on Taiwan – poetically in pouring rain – at 11.30 in the morning of February 25th 1974. Some forty other ships, all destined for the scrapyards, were waiting in the harbor. Captain ten Kate and his crew had to wait aboard until a berth was available. A week or so later, on March 2nd, word came to lift anchor and proceed to Berth 57. On the 4th, with the liner securely alongside, the captain signed the ship over to the Nan Feng Steel Company and then flew home to Amsterdam via Singapore. Some time elapsed, however, before, on May 16th, the actual dismantling began. Another once-popular liner, the *Homeric* (the former *Mariposa* of 1932), was at the adjacent slip, meeting her end as well. The two former notable liners, both especially popular and well remembered for their New York services, were reduced to rubble in sight of one another. It was an especially grim time for aging, expensive ocean liners. At about the same time, the likes of the *Orcades, Vera Cruz, Giulio*

Cesare, Chusan, Santa Maria, Orsova and the former *President Cleveland* were being broken up as well.

Later, with masts, then funnels and all lifeboats removed, the *Nieuw Amsterdam* was gradually demolished. She disappeared in sections. The breaking-up was completed on October 5th. That grand ship was gone forever.

Entering the floating dry dock at Schiedam. (Wilton-Fijenoord B. V.)

Above left: Docked in the Caribbean during a cruise. (Holland America Line)

Above right; Crossing on the Dutch flagship in a view from the port-side bridge. (Holland America Line)

Left: Getting new boilers during the major refit and repair in the summer of 1967. (Holland America Line)

Right: The *Nieuw Amsterdam* and the *Statendam* together in a painting by artist Harley Crossley. (Author's Collection)

Above left: A superb painting by Stephen J. Card. (Albert Wilhelmi Collection)

Above right: A painting by Dutch artist Willem Johan Hoendervanger.

The *Statendam* (left) and the *Nieuw Amsterdam* at the Wilhelminakade, Rotterdam. (Albert Wilhelmi Collection)

A moodful painting by Dutch artist J. Breeman. (Albert Wilhelmi Collection)

Outbound at Rotterdam with the Euromast in the foreground. (Albert Wilhelmi Collection)

Above: Festive departure – a Saturday afternoon sailing for the Caribbean. (Vincent Messina Collection)

Left: Departing from Pier 40. (Vincent Messina Collection)

The great funnels as seen in the final light of day in the Caribbean. (Vincent Messina Collection)

A view from the aft mast. (Vincent Messina Collection)

Above left: The great liner in Norway's spectacular Geirangerfjord. (Robert O'Brien Collection)

Above right: Holland America liners of the 1950s included the 15,000-ton *Maasdam*, seen here departing from Hoboken with Manhattan in the background. (Moran Towing & Transportation Co.)

Right: The outbound *Statendam* passes the inbound *Ryndam* in a midday scene at New York dating from 1960. (Gillespie-Faber Collection)

Above left: The handsome-looking *Statendam* was commissioned in February 1957. (Gillespie-Faber Collection)

Above right: A nighttime view of the *Statendam* at the Wilhelminakade. (Gillespie-Faber Collection)

Left: Busy day at Hoboken in September 1957: three American Export Line freighters are in the foreground; the *Statendam*, *Noordam* and *Maasdam* are at the Holland America Line piers; then an Anchor Line and Holland America freighter; and while the *Groote Beer* is at the 9th Street pier. (Moran Towing & Transportation Co.)

Above left: The brand-new *Rotterdam* at the 5th Street pier in a view dated September 1959. The funnel of the *Statendam* can be seen to the right. (Albert Wilhelmi Collection)

Above right: Heavy weather during a crossing aboard the *Rotterdam*. (Holland America Line)

Right: The celebrated Dutch liner *Johan van Oldenbarnevelt*, built in 1930 and normally used on the Amsterdam-Dutch East Indies run, was used for Holland America sailings in the 1950s. (Gillespie-Faber Collection)

Left: Another liner, the 20,500-ton *Oranje*, also of the Nederland Line, was looked after by the Holland America Line during her New York calls in the early 1960s. (Albert Wilhelmi Collection)

Right: The *Willem Ruys* was also handled by the Holland America Line for her visits to New York. (Albert Wilhelmi Collection)

Left: The *Groote Beer*, seen here departing from Rotterdam on September 3rd 1953, was one of three sisters (the others being the *Waterman* and *Zuiderkruis)* that provided low-fare tourist but mostly student transport on the North Atlantic. (Holland America Line)

Right: Holland America Line had a vast freighter fleet until the 1960s, which included ships such as the twelve-passenger *Sloterdyk*, seen here at the 5th Street pier in Hoboken. (Gillespie-Faber Collection)

Above left: Last rites: the glorious *Nieuw Amsterdam* being dismantled at Kaohsiung on Taiwan in the spring of 1974. (Vincent Messina Collection)

Above right: Some of the Holland America liners of the 1950s had varied endings to otherwise long careers. Here we see the *Copa Casino,* in a view at Gulfport, Mississippi dated February 4th 1996. She had been the *Ryndam* of 1951. (Peter Knego)

Left: The laid-up, rusting Greek cruise ship *Regent Star* in Eleusis Bay, Greece in 1998. She had been the *Statendam* of 1957. (Philippe Brebant Collection)

POSTSCRIPT

These days, by 2010, Holland America is bigger and better than ever. Owned by Miami-headquartered Carnival Corporation since 1988, the company – while still linked to Holland and that rich Dutch maritime heritage – has no less than fourteen modern liners. From its headquarters at Seattle, the HAL fleet is sent on cruises throughout the world, from 2 to 102 days and to up to 300 different ports. Nostalgically, on North European cruises, company liners often stop at the Wilhelminakade at Rotterdam. In July 2008, the 86,000-ton, 2,000-passenger *Eurodam* was officially named at the terminal, with the honors being done by Her Majesty Queen Beatrix, the seventy-year-old granddaughter of Queen Wilhelmina, who named the *Nieuw Amsterdam* some seventy-one years earlier, in April 1937.

2009 marked the 400th anniversary of Henry Hudson's discovery of what would become the Dutch settlement in the New World of New Amsterdam, and which then later became New York under the British.

Numerous events and exhibitions in Manhattan and along the Hudson River were organized to celebrate the anniversary. That September, the Crown Prince and Princess of the Netherlands paid a visit to New York. In the summer of 2010, the company added its largest liner yet, the 87,000-ton, 2,100-passenger, Italian-built *Nieuw Amsterdam*. Thoughtfully, her interiors pay homage to New York.

It is in partial tribute to its great history and grand ships that Holland America's next liner, the largest yet in the fleet, will be named *Nieuw Amsterdam*. More than any other, she honors of the glorious career of the well-remembered 'Darling of the Dutch'. The naming is also in tribute to the company's long link with New York City, the island of Manhattan, which began, in 1609, as the Dutch settlement known as New Amsterdam. The Dutch had created much history and one of the highlights was the creation of the *Nieuw Amsterdam* of 1938, one of the most beautiful and beloved liners ever to sail. Three long blasts to the 'Darling of the Dutch'!

The *Nieuw Amsterdam* outward bound from Southampton on August 12, 1964, from Rotterdam to New York. (J&C McCutcheon Collection)

BIBLIOGRAPHY

Braynard, Frank O. *Lives of the Liners*. New York: Cornell Maritime Press, 1947.

Braynard, Frank O. & William H. Miller. *Fifty Famous Liners*, Volumes 1-3. Cambridge, England: Patrick Stephens Ltd, 1982-86.

Cassidy, Thomas (editor). *Ocean & Cruise News* (1980-2009). Northport, New York: World Ocean & Cruise Society.

Charles, Roland W. *Troopships of World War II*. Washington, D. C.: Army Transportation Association, 1947.

Haws, Duncan. *Merchant Fleets: Holland America Line*. Uckfield, England: T. C. L. Publications, 1995.

Mayes, William. *Cruise Ships* (second edition). Windsor, England: Overview Press Ltd, 2007.

Miller, William H. *The Cruise Ships*. London, England: Conway Maritime Press Ltd, 1988.

--- *The Last Atlantic Liners*. London, England: Conway Maritime Press Ltd, 1985.

Plowman, Peter. *Emigrant Ships to Luxury Liners*. Kensington, Australia: New South Wales University Press, 1992.

Squarey, C. M. *The Patient Talks*. London: Thomas Cook & Son Ltd, 1955.

Williams, David & Richard P. De Kerbrech. *Damned by Destiny*. Brighton, England: Teredo Books, 1982.

Ships Monthly. Burton-on-Trent, England: Waterway Productions Ltd, 1982-2000.

Towline (1950-1998). New York: Moran Towing & Transportation Co.

The *Nieuw Amsterdam* from the air. (J&C McCutcheon Collection)